NATIONAL GEOGRAPHIC
School Publishing

Wind, Water, and Sunlight

Nisha Da Silva

PICTURE CREDITS
Cover, 2, 4 (above right, below right), 5 (all), 6, 7 (all), 8 (all), 9 (above left, below left, below right), 10, 12, 13 (above left, above right, below right), 14 (all), 17 (all), 18 (all), 19 (right), Photolibrary.com; 1, 15, Pavel Filatov/Alamy; 4 (left), John E. Marriott/Alamy; 9 (above right), 11 (all), 13 (below left), 16, 19 (left), Getty Images.

Produced through the worldwide resources of the National Geographic Society, John M. Fahey, Jr., President and Chief Executive Officer; Gilbert M. Grosvenor, Chairman of the Board; Nina D. Hoffman, Executive Vice President and President, Books and Education Publishing Group.

PREPARED BY NATIONAL GEOGRAPHIC SCHOOL PUBLISHING
Steve Mico, Executive Vice President and Publisher, Children's Books and Education Publishing Group; Marianne Hiland, Editor in Chief; Lynnette Brent, Executive Editor; Michael Murphy and Barbara Wood, Senior Editors; Nicole Rouse, Editor; Bea Jackson, Design Director; David Dumo, Art Director; Shanin Glenn, Designer; Margaret Sidlosky, Illustrations Director; Matt Wascavage, Manager of Publishing Services; Sean Philpotts, Production Manager.

MANUFACTURING AND QUALITY MANAGEMENT
Christopher A. Liedel, Chief Financial Officer; Phillip L. Schlosser, Vice President; Clifton M. Brown III, Director.

BOOK DEVELOPMENT
Ibis for Kids Australia Pty Limited.

Published by the National Geographic Society
1145 17th Street, N.W.
Washington, D.C. 20036-4688

Product No. 4W1005056

ISBN-13: 978-1-4263-5052-8
ISBN-10: 1-4263-5052-X

2017
5 6 7 8 9 10 11 12 13 14 15

Printed in the United States of America

Contents

Think and Discuss

How do wind, water, and sunlight change things in nature?

How do people use the power of wind, water, and sunlight?

ocean

surfers

solar-powered car

The Power of Wind

Wind can make things move.
Wind can change things.
How do we see the **power** of wind in nature?

The force of the wind makes this tree grow sideways.

These sand dunes are shaped by the wind.

The wind scatters the seeds of this milkweed plant.

How do people use the power of wind?

People use wind to help dry clothes.

Wind makes a kite fly.

People use windmills to make electricity.

Wind makes a sailboat move.

Did You Know?

Wind is air that is moving. People, plants, and animals need air to survive.

The Power of Water

Water can make things move.
Water can change things.
How do we see the power of water in nature?

The Colorado River washed away rocks and soil for millions of years. This made the Grand Canyon.

These waves are shaping the rocky cliffs.

This fast river is moving soil and making rocks smooth.

How do people use the power of water?

People use water from this dam to make electricity.

Water helps move this boat along the river.

Water makes the wheels turn on this mill. The waterwheels help grind wheat into flour.

Did You Know?

Water is needed for life. People, plants, and animals need water to survive.

The Power of Sunlight

Sunlight can make things change.
How do we see the power of sunlight in nature?

Heat from the sun **melts** the ice on this river.

How do people use the power of sunlight?

Power from the sun makes this car move.

People use sunlight to make this telephone work.

People can use sunlight to dry tomatoes.

Use What You Learned

tornado

dry mud

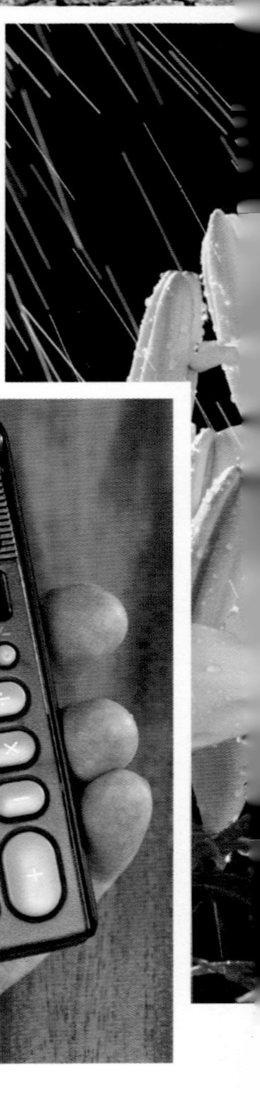

solar-powered calculator

Talk about these pictures.

How do they show the power of wind, water, and sunlight?

heat

melts

power

sunlight

water

wind

Picture Glossary

dam

sand dunes

seeds

solar-powered car

waterwheel

windmills